We're from
Greece

Victoria Parker

Welcome to Greece!

Heinemann LIBRARY

young Explorer

www.heinemann.co.uk/library
Visit our website to find out more information about **Heinemann Library** books.

To order:
 Phone 44 (0) 1865 888066
 Send a fax to 44 (0) 1865 314091
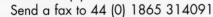 Visit the Heinemann Bookshop at www.heinemann.co.uk/library to browse our catalogue and order online.

First published in Great Britain by Heinemann Library, Halley Court, Jordan Hill, Oxford OX2 8EJ, part of Harcourt Education.
Heinemann is a registered trademark of Harcourt Education Ltd.

Editorial: Jilly Attwood, Kate Bellamy and Catherine Williams
Design: Ron Kamen and Celia Jones
Photographer: Fiona Freund
Picture Research: Maria Joannou
Production: Séverine Ribierre

Originated by Ambassador Litho Ltd
Printed and bound in China by South China Printing Company

ISBN 0 431 11937 6
09 08 07 06 05
10 9 8 7 6 5 4 3 2 1

British Library Cataloguing in Publication Data

Parker, Victoria
We're From Greece
949. 5'076

A full catalogue record for this book is available from the British Library.

Acknowledgements

Corbis/Royalty Free pp. **4a, 4b, 30b**; European Central Bank p. **30a**; Fiona Freund pp. **1, 5a, 5b, 6, 7, 8a, 8b, 9, 10, 11, 12a, 12b, 13, 14a, 14b, 15a, 15b, 16, 17, 18a, 18b, 19, 20, 21, 22, 23a, 23b, 24, 25a, 25b, 26a, 26b, 27, 28, 29, 30c**

Cover photograph of Stephanos and his friends reproduced with permission of Fiona Freund.

Many thanks to Stefanos, Dimitria, Chrysanna and their families.

Every effort has been made to contact copyright holders of any material reproduced in this book. Any omissions will be rectified in subsequent printings if notice is given to the publishers.

The paper used to print this book comes from sustainable resources.

Contents

Where is Greece?.................................4

Meet Stefanos...............................6

At school......................................8

What is for supper?......................10

The capital city..........................12

Meet Dimitria.............................14

A big family................................16

Dimitria's day.............................18

Boats and the sea.......................20

Meet Chrysanna...........................22

Summer by the sea......................24

Celebrations..............................26

The history of Greece...................28

Greek fact file............................30

Glossary.....................................31

More books to read......................31

Index...32

Words appearing in the text in bold, **like this**, are explained in the Glossary.

 Find out more about Greece at www.heinemannexplore.co.uk

Where is Greece?

To learn about Greece we meet three children who live there. Greece is a country in Europe. It has a long coast and over 2000 islands.

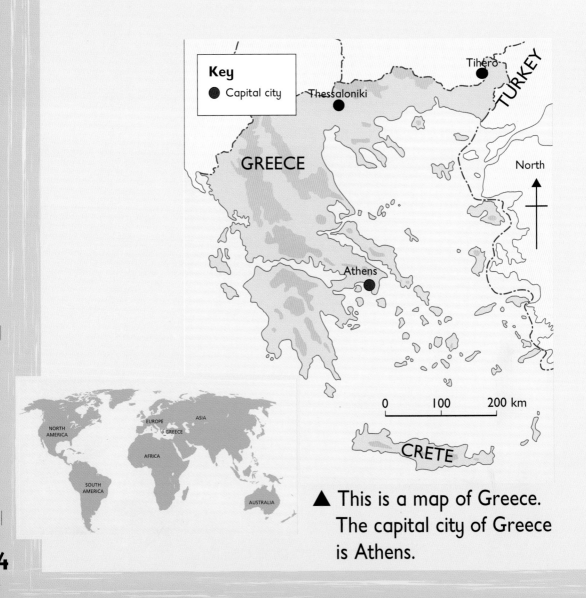

Key
● Capital city

Tihero

TURKEY

Thessaloniki

GREECE

North

Athens

0   100   200 km

CRETE

▲ This is a map of Greece. The capital city of Greece is Athens.

NORTH AMERICA

EUROPE
ASIA
GREECE

AFRICA

SOUTH AMERICA

AUSTRALIA

Greece has many hills and mountains.
It is sunny and hot for most of the
year. In the winter it rains. Sometimes
it even snows.

Meet Stefanos

Stefanos is seven years old. He comes from a city called Thessaloniki. He lives with his parents and his younger brother, Dimitris.

Stefanos's father is a businessman. His mother runs a shop. The family live in a modern flat with a **balcony**.

Stefanos's mother

Stefanos's father

Stefanos

Dimitris

7

At school

Stefanos goes to school five days a week. School starts at half past eight and finishes at half past one. His lessons are in Greek. He is starting to learn English, too.

At break, Stefanos loves playing basketball. He enjoys lots of sports, like football and swimming.

What is for supper?

Stefanos's mother goes to the market to buy food. Thessaloniki is by the sea so the market has lots of fresh fish. It also sells fruit and vegetables that are grown in the countryside nearby.

Many Greek meals are lots of small dishes, called *mezze*. Stefanos likes eating vine leaves stuffed with lamb and rice.

The capital city

The capital city of Greece is Athens. It is in the south of the country. It is a very busy place because lots of people live there.

These soldiers are guarding the
Greek **parliament** buildings in
Athens. They are wearing national
dress. Greek people often wear
national dress at **festivals**.

Meet Dimitria

Dimitria is eight years old. She lives in a farming village in northern Greece. She lives with her parents and two older sisters.

Despina

Evangelia

Dimitria's father

Dimitria

Dimitria's mother

On their farm, Dimitria's family grow **sugar beets**, **cotton**, tomatoes and watermelons. They also keep some chickens.

▼ Picking cotton is a messy business!

A big family

Dimitria's grandparents live near her. She sees them every day. Her grandmother taught her mother to make lace. Now Dimitria is learning too.

Dimitria has lots of uncles, aunts and cousins who live nearby. They often see each other at big family meals.

▲ One uncle and aunt run a shop in the village.

Dimitria's day

Dimitria goes to school five days a week. Every night she has three hours of homework. She also has jobs to do for her family.

▼ Dimitria helps to look after her grandmother's goats.

18

On Sundays, Dimitria goes to church.
She says prayers and lights a candle.
Afterwards, her family go out
together for a meal.

19

Boats and the sea

There are all sorts of boats on the sea around Greece. Some are used for sailing or fishing. Some are used to move goods from place to place.

▼ These big ships are off the coast of Athens.

Many people who live on Greek islands have their own boat. It can be easier to travel by sea than to drive over the rocky land.

Meet Chrysanna

Chrysanna is eight years old. She lives with her parents and her three brothers. Chrysanna's family live on a large Greek island called Crete.

Chrysanna's father

Nikolas

Chrysanna's mother

Epaminoudas

Orestis

Chrysanna

▲ Chrysanna's family are having lunch in a restaurant.

Chrysanna's family live in a flat in a seaside town. There are orange and **olive** trees near Chrysanna's home.

23

Summer by the sea

Lots of people come to Crete for their summer holidays. Chrysanna's town is filled with **guesthouses**, restaurants and cafés.

Chrysanna's parents own a big hotel next to the beach. Chrysanna helps out in the school holidays.

Celebrations

Today, it is the name day of Chrysanna's best friend. This is the feast day of the **Christian saint** her friend is named after. Name days are even more important than birthdays!

▲ Time for a party!

At parties, people often do **traditional** dances to Greek music. Chrysanna and her friends are very good at traditional dancing. They learn it at school.

The history of Greece

The people who lived in Greece
a long time ago are called the
Ancient Greeks. They built many big,
important cities. You can still see
bits of them today.

▲ The Ancient Greeks made this building
on a hill above Athens.

◀ The Ancient Greeks held plays in this outdoor theatre.

The Ancient Greeks had many good ideas, which we still use today. We often copy their rules, their buildings, their stories, their plays and lots more!

Greek fact file

Flag	Capital city	Money

Athens

Euros

Religion
• Most Greeks are **Orthodox** Christians. There are a few Muslims too.

Language
• The language used in Greece is called Greek. It has a different alphabet from English. The Greek alphabet only has 24 letters.

Try speaking Greek!
These Greek words are written the way they sound:

yasoo .... *hello or goodbye*
parakalo .... *please*
tee kanees .... *how are you?*

 Find out more about Greece at
www.heinemannexplore.co.uk

Glossary

balcony floor on the outside of a building usually with a wall or rail around it

Christian saint a holy person in the Christian religion

cotton a plant that can be made into cloth

festival big celebration for a town or country

guesthouse a small hotel, often run by a family

olive small green or black fruit with a stone

Orthodox an Orthodox Christian strictly follows the rules and traditions of the Christian religion

parliament the group of people who run a country

sugar beet a plant that can be made into sugar

traditional something that has been going for a very long time without changing

More books to read

Europe, Leila Merrell Foster (Heinemann Library, 2002)

What's it like to live in ... Greece?, Jillian Powell (Hodder and Stoughton, 2003)

Around the world: Schools, Margaret Hall (Heinemann Library, 2002)

Index

celebrations 26, 27

cities 4, 6, 12, 28

coasts 4, 20, 23, 25

Europe 4

food 10, 11, 15, 22

houses 7, 14, 23

land 4, 5, 21, 23

languages 8, 30

religion 19, 26, 30

school 8, 9, 18, 27

transport 20, 21

weather 5

work 7, 15, 17, 18, 25

Titles in the *We're From* series include:

Hardback   0 431 11935 X

Hardback   0 431 11932 5

Hardback   0 431 11937 6

Hardback   0 431 11933 3

Hardback   0 431 11936 8

Hardback   0 431 11934 1

Find out about the other titles in this series on our website www.heinemann.co.uk/library